One of his disciples said unto him,
"Lord, teach us to Pray"
the Bible Way

TEACH US TO PRAY

THE BIBLE WAY

Bob Bashawaty

WestBow
PRESS
A DIVISION OF THOMAS NELSON

Cover design: Nick Freidrich
Editors: Sam and Joyce Oh
Book Illustration: iStock

WestBow Press books may be ordered through booksellers or by contacting:

WestBow Press
A Division of Thomas Nelson
1663 Liberty Drive
Bloomington, IN 47403
www.westbowpress.com
1-(866) 928-1240

ISBN: 978-1-4497-1171-9 (sc)
ISBN: 978-1-4497-1170-2 (e)

Library of Congress Control Number: 2011920901

Printed in the United States of America
WestBow Press rev. date: 2/16/2011

TABLE OF CONTENTS

"The one concern of the devil is to keep Christians from praying. He fears nothing from prayerless studies, prayerless work and prayerless religion. He laughs at our toil, mocks at our wisdom, but he trembles when we pray."

Samuel Chadwick

THE PURPOSE OF THIS BOOK

The purpose of this book is to teach you to pray the Bible way. In Luke chapter eleven one of the disciples said unto Jesus, "Lord, teach us to pray" and Jesus said, "Say this" and he led them word for word through the Lord's Prayer. This amazing prayer includes the elements of adoration, confession, thanksgiving and supplication (A.C.T.S.) and establishes for us the Biblical pattern that God desires for prayer. This book is intended to lead you through those elements of prayer while still allowing you to make the prayer personal. As we follow this pattern we will use a great deal of scripture which is like praying to God in His "language". You might ask, "Is that really praying?" It is if you make the words you say your own. Just like when we sing songs of praise written by others, we make them our own because they're sung from the heart, so also, when we pray using the scripture, we don't just read the words; we make those words our own. That's the miracle of prayer.

When thoughts and words are turned toward God, you have direct access to God. So to experience the greatest benefit from these times of prayer, it's important that you keep your mind focused. Recite the words of scripture in each section and contemplate their meaning.* Then offer them up to God in prayer or, if they speak to your heart and stimulate your thoughts, offer those thoughts to God as a personal prayer. And finally, be honest with yourself and with God during the time of confession so your heart is truly right before God. Prayer is such a privilege as we enter into the very throne room of God and speak directly with him. So I encourage you to take this time seriously. Set aside all distractions and give your full attention to the Lord who is worthy. My sincere desire is that you will develop a consistent habit of prayer with God according to the pattern that Jesus gave us. May God bless you.

* Many of the Psalms of adoration are in the third person. To make these scriptures more personal, they have been changed to the first person. These verses will be identified with an asterisk *

Prayer Works

"The weapons of our warfare are not carnal but mighty through God" (KJV)

2Corinthians 10:4

Prayer is simply communication between a Father and his child but it is also the means by which Christians unleash the infinite resources of heaven. God loves it when His children pray and He uses our prayers to accomplish His purposes. When we pray properly, God hears and answers our prayers. Jeremiah 33:3 says, "Call unto me and I will answer thee and show thee great and mighty things which thou knowest not."

The Bible is filled with examples of how prayer moved the hand of God in a mighty way.

- Moses prayed and the Red sea parted. (Exodus 13 & 14) He prayed again and water came out of a rock in the desert. (Exodus 17:6)

- Hannah prayed and God granted her a child. (1Samuel 1 & 2)

- Gideon prayed and his army of 300 defeated the whole nation of Midian. (Judges 7)

- Shadrach, Meshach and Abednego prayed and were delivered from the fiery furnace. (Daniel 3)

- Daniel prayed and the mouths of lions were shut. (Daniel 6)

- Jesus prayed and fed the 5000 (Mathew 14:13-21). He prayed again and raised Lazarus from the dead (John 11).

- Peter prayed on the day of Pentecost and 3000 souls got saved (Acts 2)

- The church prayed and Peter was freed from prison (Acts 12).

These Biblical examples establish for us the value and necessity of prayer. James 5:16 says, "The effectual, fervent prayer of a righteous man availeth much." Webster defines effective as that which produces or is sufficient to produce a desired result. So then, effective prayer is that amount of proper prayer necessary to affect a result. What this means is that God in his sovereign wisdom and foreknowledge has designed in His plan the *absolute necessity* of a believer's participation by prayer in the accomplishment of His purpose and will. This is a great truth that we must accept by faith!!! So as a Christian, when the Holy Spirit burdens your heart with a specific need you are to respond with prayer, determined to pray as much and for as long as is required by God, who uses those prayers to produce His desired result.

There is a wonderful example of this reality in Daniel Chapter nine. Daniel was reading the scriptures when he realized from the writings of Jeremiah that the Babylonian captivity of the nation of Israel would come to an end in three years. This was declared in the Word of God and therefore would absolutely come to pass based on the sovereign determination of God. So what did Daniel do? He immediately went to his knees in prayer pleading with God to accomplish the deliverance of Israel. Why would he do that knowing that God's purpose would come to pass? Because Daniel understood that one of the elements used by God to fulfill His Divine purpose were his prayers.

Well then you ask, "Why does is seem that my prayers never get answered?" James tells us that we have not because we ask not... You say. "Oh no I ask a lot!!"

"We ask and do not receive because we ask for the wrong reason; that we can consume it on our own lusts." (James 4:3)

Perhaps your prayers aren't answered because you don't pray properly. Proper prayer includes several ingredients which are reflected in this book. *First*, it prepares the heart of the petitioner to come into the presence of a Holy God in dependence, humility and confession of sin. *Second,* it acknowledges the supremacy of God and desires that His Glory be displayed. *Third,* it accepts by faith the wisdom of God and thus desires only His will regarding every situation.

Prayer then for the believer is the means by which we participate with God to accomplish His will, bring Him glory, exalt his Son and become more and more conformed to the image of Jesus Christ.

One final thought: We learn to pray by praying.

"The men who have done the most for God in this world have been early on their knees. He who fritters away the early morning, its opportunity and freshness, in other pursuits than seeking God will make poor headway seeking Him the rest of the day."

E.M. Bounds

THE ELEMENTS OF PRAYER: A.C.T.S.

ADORATION

CONFESSION

THANKSGIVING

SUPPLICATION

ADORATION

In the expanse of the universe with its billions of galaxies and innumerable stars and planets, there is no greater being than God. In fact He is infinitely greater than the universe because He is its creator. By the word of the Lord the heavens were made, and by the breath of his mouth all their host (Psalms 33:6). This is why God is worthy of our adoration and praise. We have the privilege to come boldly and with confidence into His presence because of the work of Jesus Christ on our behalf but, we are also to approach God with reverence and respect.

Beginning our prayer time with adoration is appropriate because it acknowledges who God is and prepares our hearts to properly honor Him. When we begin to recite the awesome works of our creator, it makes us mindful of our absolute dependence on Him. It is He who gives us life; and even our very breath is from Him for in Him we live and move and have our being. He sustains the world we live in and supplies the air and the food and the rain we need to exist. We adore God because of His wonderful Grace and in so doing we promote within our hearts a spirit of humility. This is a crucial element of prayer because God resists the proud but gives grace to the humble. Just as we would put on our best clothes in the presence of a King or President, so we should clothe ourselves in humility every time we come into the presence of our Lord in heaven.

O praise the LORD, all ye nations; praise him, all ye people. (KJV)

Psalms 117:1

CONFESSION

Confession of sin before a Holy God in prayer is absolutely imperative if we hope to have our prayers heard. Psalms 66:18 says, "If I regard iniquity in my heart, the Lord will not hear [me]". Now clearly God, who is sovereign and knows all things, can hear you, but He is under no obligation to answer you when there is unconfessed sin in your life. If you are a follower of Jesus Christ then you are to forsake sin and pursue a life of obedience and righteousness. Since we all fail in this pursuit, God has graciously made a provision for us in 1John 1:9. "If we confess our sins, [God] is faithful and just to forgive us [our] sins and cleanse us from all unrighteousness."

The key to this promise is obviously, our confession. Confession means to acknowledge our transgression and purpose not to do it any longer. That is called repentance. We are to repent of sin as often as we commit it even if we habitually commit the same sin. God is patient and forgiving but He does require us to confess sin to receive that forgiveness. According to Psalm 51:4, all sin is ultimately against God. Therefore when we neglect to confess the sin in our lives, our relationship with Him is out of harmony. The Holy Spirit within us is grieved and eventually our conscience becomes insensitive to the extent that God hates sin. Once you become a child of God through faith alone in Jesus Christ, you will always be a child of God. That position never changes, but in order to experience the sweet communion of prayer with God, you cannot pass over this element of prayer.

I acknowledged my sin unto thee, and mine iniquity have I not hid. I said, I will confess my transgressions unto the LORD; and thou forgave the iniquity of my sin.
(KJV) Ps. 32:5

THANKSGIVING

The mark of a true child of God is a thankful heart. The Bible tells us that we are to give thanks in all circumstances, for this is the will of God in Christ Jesus for you (1Thessalonians 5:18). Not every circumstance in life is pleasant and often times they bring pain, sorrow and heartache which can easily lead to discouragement or depression or a variety of other negative emotions. The key to overcoming the burdens of life is to have a grateful heart. Most often we tend to thank God for the blessings of life; the weather, our health, job, home, family etc. and this is certainly an appropriate prayer however, it shouldn't be the primary type of thankfulness. If you examine the pattern of prayer in the Bible, you will notice that overwhelmingly, they are focused on the person of God. When we enter His gates with thanksgiving, it should be first and foremost, to express our gratitude for who God is; His character and His attributes (see page 10). Secondly, our thankfulness should focus on what God has done for us that has eternal benefit; forgiveness, salvation, adoption, spiritual gifts, heavenly inheritance etc. God is delighted when we reverently proclaim our thanks for who He is and what He has done. That's the prayer of thanksgiving.

Enter into his gates with thanksgiving, and into his courts with praise: be thankful unto him, and bless his name. (KJV)

Psalm 100:4

SUPPLICATION

God's loving desire is to supply all of our need according to His riches in glory. There is only one qualification. Everything God grants us is designed to make us more like Jesus Christ and equip us for heaven. There our no limits to His generosity when what we desire of Him will be effective in accomplishing that single minded goal. God wants us to come to him with every need and every desire but how He answers is determined by whether our request will change us into His image. Our spiritual maturity can be measured by how committed we are to cooperating with God in achieving this goal in our lives. Mathew 6:33 puts it this way, "Seek first the kingdom of God and His righteousness and all these things will be added unto you." Jesus said that a disciple of his will deny himself, take up his cross daily and follow Him (Luke 9:23). That is why when we petition God, our requests should be made in Christ's name and according to the will of God. In other words, our prayer requests should express the heart and mind of Christ and should reflect God's glory by ultimately fulfilling His divine purpose. So whether it's a personal need or intercessory prayer, in everything by prayer and supplication with thanksgiving let your requests be made known unto God.

...praying at all times in the Spirit, with all prayer and supplication. To that end keep alert with all perseverance, making supplication for all the saints... (ESV)

Eph. 6:18

GOD FROM A TO Z

A) All-knowing, Almighty, Awesome, Able
B) Benevolent, blessed, bountiful, beautiful
C) Comforter, counselor, compassionate, creator
D) Divine, dependable, destroyer, deliverer
E) Everlasting, excellent, exalted, exceptional, efficient, emancipator
F) Faithful, forgiving, Father
G) Great, gracious, good, glorious, generous
H) Holy, heavenly, humorous, healer, honest
I) Infinite, immortal, Immutable, infallible
J) Just, joyful, jealous, Jehovah
K) Kind, King
L) Loving, life, light, Lord, Longsuffering
M) Mighty, merciful, majestic, magnificent, miraculous
N) Noble, never ending
O) Omnipotent, omnipresent, omniscient
P) Patient, powerful, potentate, pure, precious, perfect
Q) Quick, quiet
R) Righteous, royal, remarkable
S) Sovereign, savior, strong, secure, steadfast
T) Tender, triumphant, timeless, truthful, trustworthy, teacher
U) Understanding, unmatched, unlimited, unique, unsearchable
V) Virtuous, victorious, vigilant, vengeful, valiant
W) Worthy, wise, wonderful, Word
X) X-rayer, Xavier (French for Savior)
Y) Yaweh,
Z) Zealous

Why not spend some time and think of other words that describe the wonder and glory of God.

THE CHALLENGE

Life is filled with challenges. From the day we are born, we are faced with challenges that need to be overcome; the challenges to roll over, crawl, walk and finally run. It's called life and by these challenges we grow stronger, develop discipline and achieve our goals.

The greatest challenge facing any of us who are followers of Jesus Christ is the problem of sin. Though the penalty of sin was paid for at the cross, the presence of sin and its allure is an ongoing struggle for every believer (Romans 7). Even so we are called upon to overcome this challenge because we are overcomers in Christ.

One of the most important weapons we have against sin (and perhaps the least used) is prayer. Starting your day with proper prayer prepares you for the battle.

My challenge to you is to begin each morning with one of the ten daily prayers in this book.

Embrace these prayers as your own and use them to connect with the resources of God to experience victory and spiritual growth in your Christian walk. Use the journaling portion of the book to make these prayers more personal and consider working through the book with a partner to keep yourself accountable to this challenge. When you've completed the ten days of prayer then begin again and continue to do so until the pattern of prayer becomes a habit of prayer. The benefits to you will be immeasurable because they are infinite and eternal.

I pray that you will **discipl**ine yourself to rise to this challenge as a **disciple** of Jesus. So let's get with it: *"knowing the time, that now it is high time to awake out of sleep: for now is our salvation nearer than when we believed."* (KJV) Romans 13:11

Day One: Adoration

P*s. 9:1-2. I will praise you, O LORD, with all my heart; I will tell of all your wonders. I will be glad and rejoice in you; I will sing praise to your name, O Most High. (NIV)*

*Ps. 18:1-2. I love you, O LORD, my strength. You, O LORD are my rock, my fortress and my deliverer; my God is my rock, in whom I take refuge. You are my shield and the horn of my salvation, my stronghold. * (ESV)*

*Ps. 18:3A, 30-31. I call to you, O LORD, who is worthy of praise. As for you, Father, your way is perfect; your word O LORD is flawless. You are a shield for all who take refuge in you. For who is God besides you, O LORD? And who is the Rock except my God? * (NIV)*

*Ps. 24:1-2 The earth is yours O LORD, and everything in it, the world, and all who live in it; for you founded it upon the seas and established it upon the waters. * (NIV)*

*Ps. 28:6-7. Praise be to you LORD, for you have heard my cry for mercy. You O LORD are my strength and my shield; my heart trusts in you, and I am helped. My heart leaps for joy and I will give thanks to you in song. * (NIV)*

If there is a word or phrase in these verses that especially speaks to your heart today, underline or highlight it and spend a few minutes meditating on its truth.

*Changed from third person to first person

Day One: Confession

Confession of your sin is necessary to remove anything that would hinder your prayers to God. Begin with a call for God's help.

Remember, O LORD, your great mercy and love, for they are from of old. According to your love remember me, for you are good, O LORD. For the sake of your name, O LORD, forgive my iniquity, though it is great. Look upon my affliction and my distress and take away all my sins. (NIV)
Ps. 25:6, 7b, 11, 18

Identifying and acknowledging your sin before God can be difficult and painful. However, that is the only path to ultimate victory. Below is a list of sins recorded in the Bible. (These are defined for you in detail on page 94). Ask God to show you which ones you struggle with and confess them to Him.

Father, I confess my sins of:

Anger	Malice	Bitterness
Greed	Covetousness	Envy
Gossip	Lying	Stealing
Murder	Fornication	Adultery
Pride	Worldliness	Boasting
Drunkenness	Gluttony	Drug Abuse
Pornography	Lust	Idolatry
Unnatural affection	Evil Thoughts	Impatience
Foul Language	Laziness	Worry
Little Faith	Sorcery	Selfishness
Contentiousness	Unforgiving	Ingratitude
Critical Spirit	Abuse	Hypocrisy
Defrauding Your Spouse		

Use the space provided below to make notes and chart your progress.

Personal Notes and Progress

_____

_____

_____

_____

_____

_____

_____

_____

There is complete forgiveness in Christ and a cleansing of all unrighteousness. Let's repeat a prayer from scripture in response to God's grace.

Ps. 19:14. May the words of my mouth and the meditation of my heart be pleasing in your sight, O LORD, my Rock and my Redeemer. (NIV)

Ps. 25:4-5. Show me your ways, O LORD, teach me your paths; guide me in your truth and teach me, for you are God my Savior, and my hope is in you all day long. (NIV)

Father, I thank you for your forgiveness in Christ and, by your Spirit, I pray you will give me a hatred for my sins and the power to repent of them.

Day One: Thanksgiving

God loves a thankful heart and there is so much to thank him for.

For His Grace: Father, thank you for your abundant Grace that saved me and is sufficient toward me for all things.

For His Mercy: Father, thank you for your mercy that spared me from judgment and protects me each day.

For His Love: Father thank you for your love for it is eternal and everlasting and never wavers. You can't love me more and you won't love me less.

For Provision: Father, thank you for your promise to supply all my need according to your riches in glory.

For Growth: Father thank you for your promise to work in me both to will and to do your good pleasure as I grow in the grace and the knowledge of my Lord Jesus Christ.

For Power: Father, thank you for your exceeding great power that is at work in me and available to me.

For Wisdom: Father, thank you for your promise to give me wisdom to understand your will and purpose when I ask in faith.

God's will is that His children give thanks in everything. 1Thess. 5:18 states that in the midst of any given situation, we are to find reason to be grateful. In other words, Count your blessings...name them one by one:

FOR WHO GOD IS:

_____

_____

_____

FOR WHAT GOD HAS DONE:

_____

_____

_____

FOR SPIRITUAL BLESSINGS:

_____

_____

_____

FOR TEMPORAL BLESSINGS:

_____

_____

_____

Day One: Supplication

Now with your heart prepared before God, let your requests be made known to Him. The Apostle John tells us that if we ask anything according to God's will, He hears us. The following is a prayer that reflects the heart of God for you, as revealed in scripture.

A Prayer for Enlightenment

Eph. 1:17-19. I do not cease to give thanks for you, making mention of you in my prayers: That the God of our Lord Jesus Christ, the Father of glory, may give to you the spirit of wisdom and revelation in the knowledge of Him, the eyes of your understanding being enlightened; that you may know what is the hope of His calling, what are the riches of the glory of His inheritance in the saints, and what is the exceeding greatness of His power toward us who believe, according to the working of His mighty power. (KJV)

Lord, I pray that you would give me the spirit of wisdom and understanding to know you intimately and to comprehend fully the hope that is mine in Christ; to see by faith the glory of my future inheritance and to experience daily the greatness of your power available to me and in me.

Record your personal requests along with the date in the space below so you can keep track of God's faithfulness.

_____

_____

_____

_____

_____

_____

_____

_____

_____

_____

_____

_____

_____

_____

"Don't pray when it rains if you don't pray when the sun shines".

Satchel Paige

"Prayer does not change the purpose of God. But prayer does change the action of God."

Chuck Smith

Day Two: Adoration

P*s. 29:1-2. I will ascribe to you, O LORD, glory and strength. I will ascribe to you the glory due your name; I will worship you LORD in the splendor of your holiness.* * *(NIV)*

Ps. 34:1-3. I will extol you O LORD at all times; your praise will always be on my lips. My soul will boast in you; let the afflicted hear and rejoice. We will glorify you LORD together; we will exalt your name forever. * *(NIV)*

Ps. 36:5-7. Your love, O LORD, reaches to the heavens, your faithfulness to the skies. Your righteousness is like the mighty mountains, your justice like the great deep. O LORD, you preserve both man and beast. How priceless is your unfailing love! Both high and low among men find refuge in the shadow of your wings. (NIV)

Ps. 57:7-11. My heart is steadfast, O God, my heart is steadfast; I will sing and make music. Awake, my soul! Awake, I will praise you, O Lord, among the nations; I will sing of you among the peoples. For great is your love, reaching to the heavens; your faithfulness reaches to the skies. Be exalted, O God, above the heavens; let your glory be over all the earth. (NIV)

If there is a word or phrase in these verses that especially speaks to your heart today, underline or highlight it and spend a few minutes meditating on its truth.

*Changed from third person to first person

DAY TWO: CONFESSION

Confession of your sin is necessary to remove anything that would hinder your prayers to God. Begin with a call for God's help.

O LORD, do not rebuke me in your anger or discipline me in your wrath. For your arrows have pierced me, and your hand has come down upon me. Because of your wrath there is no health in my body; my bones have no soundness because of my sin. My guilt has overwhelmed me. (NIV)
Ps. 38:1-4a

Identifying and acknowledging your sin before God can be difficult and painful. However, that is the only path to ultimate victory. Below is a list of sins recorded in the Bible. (These are defined for you in detail on page 94). Ask God to show you which ones you struggle with and confess them to Him.

Father, I confess my sins of:

Anger	Malice	Bitterness
Greed	Covetousness	Envy
Gossip	Lying	Stealing
Murder	Fornication	Adultery
Pride	Worldliness	Boasting
Drunkenness	Gluttony	Drug Abuse
Pornography	Lust	Idolatry
Unnatural affection	Evil Thoughts	Impatience
Foul Language	Laziness	Worry
Little Faith	Sorcery	Selfishness
Contentiousness	Unforgiving	Ingratitude
Critical Spirit	Abuse	Hypocrisy
Defrauding Your Spouse		

Use the space provided below to make notes and chart your progress.

Personal Notes and Progress

_____

_____

_____

_____

_____

_____

_____

_____

There is complete forgiveness in Christ and a cleansing of all unrighteousness. Let's repeat a prayer from scripture in response to God's grace.

Ps. 32:1,2,5. Blessed is he whose transgressions are forgiven, whose sins are covered. Blessed is the man whose sin the LORD does not count against him and in whose spirit is no deceit. Then I acknowledged my sin to you and did not cover up my iniquity. I said, "I will confess my transgressions to the LORD"; and you forgave the guilt of my sin. (NIV)

Father, I thank you for your forgiveness in Christ and, by your Spirit, I pray you will give me a hatred for my sins and the power to repent of them.

Day Two: Thanksgiving

God loves a thankful heart and there is so much to thank him for.

For Future Glory: Father, thank you for my salvation in Christ and the guarantee of future glory in heaven.

For Faithfulness to Sustain: Father, thank you for life, for in you we live and move and have our being.

For the Holy Spirit: Father, thank you for the Holy Spirit who dwells in me and gives me comfort, wisdom and guidance and is the guarantee that the work of Christ on my behalf is effective and sufficient.

For His Creation: Father, thank you for the beauty and the majesty of our world; the mountains and the seas and the forests and the plains. Thank you for the heavens; the sun the moon, the stars in the night skies and all the other amazing celestial bodies.

For His Word: Father, thank you for your precious Word which you gave to us for wisdom and guidance, comfort and joy. Help me to love it more than gold or silver. Help me to spend time in your Word daily to transform my thinking and Lord, give me the faith to embrace its truths so much that it governs every moment of my day.

For His Comfort: Father, thank you for your Divine comfort which is available to me during my times of grief and for the shelter of your loving arms that are there to patiently console me throughout my difficulty.

God's will is that His children give thanks in everything. 1Thess. 5:18 states that in the midst of any given situation, we are to find reason to be grateful. In other words, Count your blessings...name them one by one:

FOR WHO GOD IS:

_____

_____

_____

FOR WHAT GOD HAS DONE:

_____

_____

_____

FOR SPIRITUAL BLESSINGS:

_____

_____

_____

FOR TEMPORAL BLESSINGS:

_____

_____

_____

DAY TWO: SUPPLICATION

Now with your heart prepared before God, let your requests be made known to Him. The Apostle John tells us that if we ask anything according to God's will, He hears us. The following is a prayer that reflects the heart of God for you, as revealed in scripture.

A Prayer for oneness with God

John 17:8-11. [Father] I have given them the words that you gave me, and they have received them and have come to know in truth that I came from you; and they have believed that you sent me. I am praying for them whom you have given me, for they are yours. All mine are yours, and yours are mine, and I am glorified in them. And I am no longer in the world, but they are in the world, and I am coming to you. Holy Father, keep them in your name, which you have given me that they may be one, even as we are one. (ESV)

Lord, I thank you that Jesus Christ, your son, is fully God manifest in the flesh and that you gave me the faith to believe in him for my salvation. I thank you that my union with Jesus unites me with you and grants me the privilege of calling you Father. I pray for your divine power to protect me from the enticements of the world and the temptations of the flesh. Lead me in a way that reflects your person and displays your glory to the degree that it draws men to the cross.

Record your personal requests along with the date in the space below so you can keep track of God's faithfulness.

_____

_____

_____

_____

_____

_____

_____

_____

_____

_____

_____

_____

_____

_____

_____

"If I could hear Christ praying for me in the next room, I would not fear a million enemies. Yet distance makes no difference. He is praying for me."

Robert Murray McCheyne

"Faith in a prayer-hearing God will make a prayer-loving Christian."

Andrew Murray

Day Three: Adoration

P*s. 62:1,6-8. My soul finds rest in You alone; my salvation comes from you, O Lord. You alone are my rock and my salvation; you are my fortress, I will not be shaken. My salvation and my honor depend on you Father; you are my mighty rock, my refuge. I will trust in you at all times. I call on all people to pour out their hearts to you, for you, O God are our refuge.* * (NIV)*

Ps. 63:1-5, 7-8. O God, you are my God, earnestly I seek you; my soul thirsts for you, my body longs for you, in a dry and weary land where there is no water. I have seen you in the sanctuary and beheld your power and your glory. (NIV)

Ps. 63:3-8. Because your love is better than life, my lips will glorify you. I will praise you as long as I live, and in your name I will lift up my hands. My soul will be satisfied as with the richest of foods; with singing lips my mouth will praise you. Because you are my help, I sing in the shadow of your wings. My soul clings to you; your right hand upholds me. (NIV)

If there is a word or phrase in these verses that especially speaks to your heart today, underline or highlight it and spend a few minutes meditating on its truth.

*Changed from third person to first person

Day Three: Confession

Confession of your sin is necessary to remove anything that would hinder your prayers to God. Begin with a call for God's help.

I wait for you, O LORD; you will answer, O Lord my God. I confess my iniquity; I am troubled by my sin. O LORD, do not forsake me; be not far from me, O my God. Come quickly to help me, O Lord my Savior. Ps. 38:15, 18, 21-22 (NIV)

Identifying and acknowledging your sin before God can be difficult and painful. However, that is the only path to ultimate victory. Below is a list of sins recorded in the Bible. (These are defined for you in detail on page 94). Ask God to show you which ones you struggle with and confess them to Him.

Father, I confess my sins of:

Anger	Malice	Bitterness
Greed	Covetousness	Envy
Gossip	Lying	Stealing
Murder	Fornication	Adultery
Pride	Worldliness	Boasting
Drunkenness	Gluttony	Drug Abuse
Pornography	Lust	Idolatry
Unnatural affection	Evil Thoughts	Impatience
Foul Language	Laziness	Worry
Little Faith	Sorcery	Selfishness
Contentiousness	Unforgiving	Ingratitude
Critical Spirit	Abuse	Hypocrisy
Defrauding Your Spouse		

Use the space provided below to make notes and chart your progress.

Personal Notes and Progress

_____

_____

_____

_____

_____

_____

_____

_____

There is complete forgiveness in Christ and a cleansing of all unrighteousness. Let's repeat a prayer from scripture in response to God's grace.

Ps. 51:10, 12, 17. Create in me a pure heart, O God, and renew a steadfast spirit within me. Restore to me the joy of your salvation and grant me a willing spirit, to sustain me. The sacrifices of God are a broken spirit; a broken and contrite heart, O God, you will not despise. (NIV)

Father, I thank you for your forgiveness in Christ and, by your Spirit, I pray you will give me a hatred for my sins and the power to repent of them.

Day Three: Thanksgiving

God loves a thankful heart and there is so much to thank him for.

For His Presence: Father, thank you for your promise to never leave me or forsake me; no matter what the circumstance, no matter what my failures, you are always there to sustain me with your loving arms.

For our victory in Christ: Father, thank you for the victory that Jesus Christ has over sin that is mine by faith. Thank you that I have the power to overcome any temptation because in Him I am more than a conqueror.

For the Forgiveness of sin: Father, thank you for the precious truth of total forgiveness of sin through Jesus Christ. I stand in your Grace so that all my sin, past, present and FUTURE are washed by His blood and are cast into the depths of the sea.

For God's infinite Patience: Father, thank you for your patience which never grows weary with my shortcomings, my failures or my lack of faithfulness but instead tenderly leads me down the path of righteousness.

For Miracles: Father, thank you for the miracles that I see around me every day. Your hand is evident in the rising of the sun, in the lilies of the field, in the birth of every living creature and the healing of disease but most of all, in the changed lives of those who receive Jesus into their hearts as Savior and Lord.

God's will is that His children give thanks in everything. 1 Thess. 5:18 states that in the midst of any given situation, we are to find reason to be grateful. In other words, Count your blessings...name them one by one:

FOR WHO GOD IS:

_____

_____

_____

FOR WHAT GOD HAS DONE:

_____

_____

_____

FOR SPIRITUAL BLESSINGS:

_____

_____

_____

FOR TEMPORAL BLESSINGS:

_____

_____

_____

Day Three: Supplication

Now with your heart prepared before God, let your requests be made known to Him. The Apostle John tells us that if we ask anything according to God's will, He hears us. The following is a prayer that reflects the heart of God for you, as revealed in scripture.

A Prayer for Sanctification

Col. 1:9-11. We ask that you may be filled with the knowledge of His will in all wisdom and spiritual understanding; that you may walk worthy of the Lord, fully pleasing Him, being fruitful in every good work and increasing in the knowledge of God; strengthened with all might, according to His glorious power, for all patience and longsuffering with joy. (NKJV)

Lord, I pray that I would know your will, understand and apply it to my life. I pray that my Christian walk would please you fully and that you might bless me in every good work. I pray that I would continue to increase in my knowledge of you, grow stronger in my faith and persevere through all trials with joy and patience.

Record your personal requests along with the date in the space below so you can keep track of God's faithfulness.

_____

_____

_____

_____

_____

_____

_____

_____

_____

_____

_____

_____

_____

_____

_____

"Don't pray when you feel like it. Have an appointment with the Lord and keep it. A man is powerful on his knees."

Corrie ten Boom

"The battle of prayer is against two things in the earthlies: wandering thoughts and lack of intimacy with God's character as revealed in His word. Neither can be cured at once, but they can be cured by discipline."

Oswald Chambers

Day Four: Adoration

Ps. 66:1-4. I will shout with joy to you O God with all the earth! I will sing the glory of your name and make your praise glorious! I will say to you, "How awesome are your deeds! So great is your power that your enemies cringe before you. All the earth bows down to you; they sing praise to you, they sing praise to your name." * (NIV)

Ps. 71: 1, 15, 16,19,23,24. In you, O Lord, I have taken refuge; my mouth will tell of your righteousness, of your salvation all day long, though I know not its measure. I will come and proclaim your mighty acts, O Sovereign LORD; I will proclaim your righteousness, yours alone. Your righteousness reaches to the skies, O God, you who have done great things. Who, O God, is like you? My lips will shout for joy when I sing praise to you; I, whom you have redeemed. My tongue will tell of your righteous acts all day long. (NIV)

Ps. 73:25-26. Who have I in heaven but you? And earth has nothing I desire besides you. My flesh and my heart may fail, but you, dear LORD are the strength of my soul and my portion forever. * (NIV)

If there is a word or phrase in these verses that especially speaks to your heart today, underline or highlight it and spend a few minutes meditating on its truth.

*Changed from third person to first person

DAY FOUR: CONFESSION

Confession of your sin is necessary to remove anything that would hinder your prayers to God. Begin with a call for God's help.

Have mercy on me, O God, according to your unfailing love; according to your great compassion blot out my transgressions. Wash away all my iniquity and cleanse me from my sin. For I know my transgressions, and my sin is always before me. Against you, you only, have I sinned and done what is evil in your sight, so that you are proved right when you speak and justified when you judge. Ps. 51:1-4 (NIV)

Identifying and acknowledging your sin before God can be difficult and painful. However, that is the only path to ultimate victory. Below is a list of sins recorded in the Bible. (These are defined for you in detail on page 94). Ask God to show you which ones you struggle with and confess them to Him.

Father, I confess my sins of:

Anger	Malice	Bitterness
Greed	Covetousness	Envy
Gossip	Lying	Stealing
Murder	Fornication	Adultery
Pride	Worldliness	Boasting
Drunkenness	Gluttony	Drug Abuse
Pornography	Lust	Idolatry
Unnatural affection	Evil Thoughts	Impatience
Foul Language	Laziness	Worry
Little Faith	Sorcery	Selfishness
Contentiousness	Unforgiving	Ingratitude
Critical Spirit	Abuse	Hypocrisy
Defrauding Your Spouse		

Use the space provided below to make notes and chart your progress.

Personal Notes and Progress

There is complete forgiveness in Christ and a cleansing of all unrighteousness. Let's repeat a prayer from scripture in response to God's grace.

Ps.86:11-16A. Teach me your way, O LORD, and I will walk in your truth; give me an undivided heart, that I may fear your name. I will praise you, O Lord my God, with all my heart; I will glorify your name forever. For great is your love toward me; you have delivered me from the depths of the grave. You, O Lord, are a compassionate and gracious God, slow to anger, abounding in love and faithfulness. Turn to me and have mercy on me; grant your strength to your servant. (NIV)

Father, I thank you for your forgiveness in Christ and, by your Spirit, I pray you will give me a hatred for my sins and the power to repent of them.

DAY FOUR: THANKSGIVING

God loves a thankful heart and there is so much to thank him for.

For His Immutability: Father, thank you for your unchanging nature; that you are the same yesterday, today and forever and thus can be relied on with absolute assurance to act according to your Holy character.

For Eternal Treasure: Father, thank you for the treasure that is laid up for me in heaven; a treasure that I can add to as I seek your kingdom and serve you with the right attitude and the right motive.

For Joy: Father, thank you for a joy unspeakable that is deep within my spirit; a joy that is not affected by circumstance but is directly related to my confidence and trust in your sovereign love.

For freedom to choose right: Father, thank you that the bondage I had to sin is broken at the cross so I can now choose to yield to the power of the Holy Spirit and walk in obedience to your commands and your will.

For Peace: Father, thank you for your peace that guards my heart and mind during the storms of life. Thank you that I can experience your peace whenever I draw close to you in prayer and supplication.

For Prayer: Father, thank you for the incredible privilege of prayer that empowers me to come boldly and with confidence right into your very presence to speak with you without fear and to know that you hear me and desire to answer my every request.

God's will is that His children give thanks in everything. 1Thess. 5:18 states that in the midst of any given situation, we are to find reason to be grateful. In other words, Count your blessings...name them one by one:

FOR WHO GOD IS:

_____

_____

_____

FOR WHAT GOD HAS DONE:

_____

_____

_____

FOR SPIRITUAL BLESSINGS:

_____

_____

_____

FOR TEMPORAL BLESSINGS:

_____

_____

_____

Day Four: Supplication

Now with your heart prepared before God, let your requests be made known to Him. The Apostle John tells us that if we ask anything according to God's will, He hears us. The following is a prayer that reflects the heart of God for you, as revealed in scripture.

A Prayer for Fruitfulness

Psalm 15. LORD, who may dwell in your sanctuary? Who may live on your holy hill? He whose walk is blameless and who does what is righteous, who speaks the truth from his heart and has no slander on his tongue, who does his neighbor no wrong and casts no slur on his fellowman, who despises a vile man but honors those who fear the LORD, who keeps his oath even when it hurts, who lends his money without usury and does not accept a bribe against the innocent. He who does these things will never be shaken. (NIV)

Lord, I pray that I would manifest the fruit of salvation in my daily walk. As a new creation in Christ, I am dead to sin and free to serve righteousness. May the words I speak reflect a pure heart that desires only to edify. May I love my neighbor as myself, speak ill of no man and rejoice in the fellowship of other believers. Lord, help me to be a good steward of my resources so I may be generous in my giving and help me to be vigilant to guard my integrity. I ask these things so that my life may draw others to a saving knowledge of my Lord Jesus Christ to the glory of my heavenly Father.

Record your personal requests along with the date in the space below so you can keep track of God's faithfulness.

_____

_____

_____

_____

_____

_____

_____

_____

_____

_____

_____

_____

_____

_____

"The little estimate we put on prayer is evidence from the little time we give to it."

E.M. Bounds

"Prayer does not fit us for the greater work; prayer is the greater work."

Oswald Chambers.

"The Lord Jesus will every day from heaven continue His work in me. But on one condition—the soul must give Him time each day to impart His love and his grace. Time alone with the Lord Jesus each day is the indispensable condition of growth and power."

Andrew Murray

DAY FIVE: ADORATION

P*s. 84:1, 2, 4, 10-12. How lovely is your dwelling place, O LORD Almighty! My soul yearns, even faints, for your court; my heart and my flesh cry out for you, O living God. O Lord Almighty, my King and my God, Blessed are those who dwell in your house; they are ever praising you. Better is one day in your courts than a thousand elsewhere; I would rather be a doorkeeper in your house gracious Father than to dwell in the tents of the wicked. For you LORD God are a sun and shield; you bestow favor and honor; no good thing do you withhold from me when my walk is blameless. O LORD Almighty, blessed am I when I trust in you. * (NIV)*

Ps.89: 1, 2, 5-8, 11-15. I will sing of your great love forever, O Lord; with my mouth I will make your faithfulness known through all generations. I will declare that your love stands firm forever, that you established your faithfulness in heaven itself. The heavens praise your wonders, O LORD, your faithfulness too, in the assembly of the holy ones. For who in the skies above can compare with you LORD? Who is like you among the heavenly beings? In the council of the holy ones you are greatly feared; you are more awesome than all who surround you. * (NIV)

If there is a word or phrase in these verses that especially speaks to your heart today, underline or highlight it and spend a few minutes meditating on its truth.

*Changed from third person to first person

DAY FIVE: CONFESSION

Confession of your sin is necessary to remove anything that would hinder your prayers to God. Begin with a call for God's help.

Help us, O God our Savior, for the glory of your name; deliver us and forgive our sins for your name's sake. Save me, O God, by your name; vindicate me by your might. Hear my prayer, O God; listen to the words of my mouth. (NIV) Ps.79:9; Ps.54:1-2

Identifying and acknowledging your sin before God can be difficult and painful. However, that is the only path to ultimate victory. Below is a list of sins recorded in the Bible. (These are defined for you in detail on page 94). Ask God to show you which ones you struggle with and confess them to Him.

Father, I confess my sins of:

Anger	Malice	Bitterness
Greed	Covetousness	Envy
Gossip	Lying	Stealing
Murder	Fornication	Adultery
Pride	Worldliness	Boasting
Drunkenness	Gluttony	Drug Abuse
Pornography	Lust	Idolatry
Unnatural affection	Evil Thoughts	Impatience
Foul Language	Laziness	Worry
Little Faith	Sorcery	Selfishness
Contentiousness	Unforgiving	Ingratitude
Critical Spirit	Abuse	Hypocrisy
Defrauding Your Spouse		

Use the space provided below to make notes and chart your progress.

Personal Notes and Progress

_____

_____

_____

_____

_____

_____

_____

_____

There is complete forgiveness in Christ and a cleansing of all unrighteousness. Let's repeat a prayer from scripture in response to God's grace.

Ps.103:8, 10-13. The LORD is compassionate and gracious; slow to anger, abounding in love. He does not treat us as our sins deserve or repay us according to our iniquities. For as high as the heavens are above the earth, so great is his love for those who fear him; as far as the east is from the west, so far has he removed our transgressions from us. As a father has compassion on his children, so the LORD has compassion on those who fear him. (NIV)

Father, I thank you for your forgiveness in Christ and, by your Spirit, I pray you will give me a hatred for my sins and the power to repent of them.

DAY FIVE: THANKSGIVING

G od loves a thankful heart and there is so much to thank him for.

For the Cross: Father, thank you for the cross of Jesus Christ. For Him it meant pain and agony and separation from you. For me it means salvation, the forgiveness of sin and eternal life.

For Jesus Christ: Father, thank you for your son Jesus Christ who set aside his glory, took on the form of a man, lived a pure and holy life then freely became sin for me that I might be made righteous in your eyes.

For the Resurrection: Father, thank you for the miracle of the resurrection of Jesus Christ from the dead which is the proof of His victory over sin, death and Satan and establishes Him as the captain of my salvation.

For Union with Christ: Father, thank you for the spiritual reality of my union with Christ; that He is in me and I am in Him, a member of his body, joined with him in His death, burial and resurrection and seated with Him in the heavenlies.

For Spiritual Gifts: Father, thank you for the spiritual gift that the Holy Spirit has imparted to me that is unique to me and gives me the divine enablement to serve the purpose of Christ.

For Understanding: Father, thank you for the ability to comprehend your truth beyond simple knowledge of the facts, but to have wisdom and spiritual understanding regarding your purpose and intent.

God's will is that His children give thanks in everything. 1Thess. 5:18 states that in the midst of any given situation, we are to find reason to be grateful. In other words, Count your blessings…name them one by one:

FOR WHO GOD IS:

_____

_____

_____

FOR WHAT GOD HAS DONE:

_____

_____

_____

FOR SPIRITUAL BLESSINGS:

_____

_____

_____

FOR TEMPORAL BLESSINGS:

_____

_____

_____

Day Five: Supplication

Now with your heart prepared before God, let your requests be made known to Him. The Apostle John tells us that if we ask anything according to God's will, He hears us. The following is a prayer that reflects the heart of God for you, as revealed in scripture.

A Prayer for Unity in the Body

John 17:20-23. [I Pray] for those who will believe in me through the [Gospel], that they may all be one, just as you, Father, are in me, and I in you, that they also may be in us, so that the world may believe that you have sent me. The glory that you have given me I have given to them, that they may be one even as we are one, I in them and you in me, that they may become perfectly one, so that the world may know that you sent me and loved them even as you loved me. (ESV)

O Lord, help me to understand the reality of my identification with Jesus. Baptized into his death and burial and raised to walk in newness of life! Father, your glory is revealed in my regeneration and transformation. And, my life of obedience by the power of the Holy Spirit is a declaration of your divine seed implanted within my heart. I pray that the desire to be one with you would dominate my soul and that desire would reflect itself in every relationship, every conversation and every opportunity I have to serve the Kingdom of Heaven.

Record your personal requests along with the date in the space below so you can keep track of God's faithfulness.

_____

_____

_____

_____

_____

_____

_____

_____

_____

_____

_____

_____

_____

_____

_____

_____

"...True prayer is measured by weight, not by length. A single groan before God may have more fullness of prayer in it than a fine oration of great length."

C. H. Spurgeon

"Time spent alone with God is not wasted. It changes us; it changes our surroundings; and every Christian who would live the life that counts, and who would have power for service must take time to pray."

M.E. Andross

Day Six: Adoration

P*s. 89:8, 11, 12A, 13-15. O LORD God Almighty, who is like you? You are mighty, O LORD, and your faithfulness surrounds you. The heavens are yours, and yours also the earth; you founded the world and all that is in it. You created the north and the south; your arm is endued with power; your hand is strong, your right hand exalted. Righteousness and justice are the foundation of your throne; love and faithfulness go before you. Blessed are those who have learned to acclaim you, who walk in the light of your presence, O LORD. (NIV)*

Ps.92:1, 2, 4, 5, 8. It is good for me to praise you LORD and make music to your name, O Most High; to proclaim your love in the morning and your faithfulness at night, For you make me glad by your deeds, O LORD; I sing for joy at the works of your hands. How great are your works, O LORD, how profound your thoughts! You O Lord, are exalted forever. * (NIV)

If there is a word or phrase in these verses that especially speaks to your heart today, underline or highlight it and spend a few minutes meditating on its truth.

*Changed from third person to first person

Day Six: Confession

Confession of your sin is necessary to remove anything that would hinder your prayers to God. Begin with a call for God's help.

If you, O LORD, kept a record of sins, O Lord, who could stand? But with you there is forgiveness; therefore you are feared. I wait for the LORD, my soul waits, and in his word I put my hope. My soul waits for the Lord for with the LORD is unfailing love and with him is full redemption. Ps. 130:3-7 (NIV)

Identifying and acknowledging your sin before God can be difficult and painful. However, that is the only path to ultimate victory. Below is a list of sins recorded in the Bible. (These are defined for you in detail on page 94). Ask God to show you which ones you struggle with and confess them to Him.

Father, I confess my sins of:

Anger	Malice	Bitterness
Greed	Covetousness	Envy
Gossip	Lying	Stealing
Murder	Fornication	Adultery
Pride	Worldliness	Boasting
Drunkenness	Gluttony	Drug Abuse
Pornography	Lust	Idolatry
Unnatural affection	Evil Thoughts	Impatience
Foul Language	Laziness	Worry
Little Faith	Sorcery	Selfishness
Contentiousness	Unforgiving	Ingratitude
Critical Spirit	Abuse	Hypocrisy
Defrauding Your Spouse		

Use the space provided below to make notes and chart your progress.

Personal Notes and Progress

There is complete forgiveness in Christ and a cleansing of all unrighteousness. Let's repeat a prayer from scripture in response to God's grace.

Ps. 30:4, 5, 11, 12. Sing to the LORD, you saints of his; praise his holy name. For his anger lasts only a moment, but his favor lasts a lifetime; weeping may remain for a night, but rejoicing comes in the morning. You turned my wailing into dancing; you removed my sackcloth and clothed me with joy, that my heart may sing to you and not be silent. O LORD my God, I will give you thanks forever. (NIV)

Father, I thank you for your forgiveness in Christ and, by your Spirit, I pray you will give me a hatred for my sins and the power to repent of them.

DAY SIX: THANKSGIVING

God loves a thankful heart and there is so much to thank him for.

For Intercession: Father, thank you for the High Priestly ministry of Jesus Christ who is holy, blameless and undefiled and ever lives to intercede for me against the accusations of the Devil.

For Freedom from sin: Father, thank you for freedom from the penalty, the guilt and the bondage of sin in my life because Jesus paid the price for me at Calvary.

For Sanctification: Father, thank you for your declaration that I have been set apart for your holy purpose through the work of the Spirit who leads me in the process of becoming by experience what I already possess fully in Christ.

For Reconciliation: Father, thank you for reconciling me to yourself by the blood of Jesus Christ. I was once your enemy now I am at peace with you and I am holy, blameless and unreproveable in your sight.

For the mind of Christ: Father, thank you for giving me the mind of Christ; a mind of humility and wisdom, peace and love; a mind that is able to know the things that are freely given to me by you and desires only to do your will.

For the Fruit of the Spirit: Father, thank you for the fruit that is produced by Your Spirit that desires to make melody in my heart and fill me with singing as I allow it to control my thoughts and motives.

God's will is that His children give thanks in everything. 1Thess. 5:18 states that in the midst of any given situation, we are to find reason to be grateful. In other words, Count your blessings...name them one by one:

FOR WHO GOD IS:

_____

_____

_____

FOR WHAT GOD HAS DONE:

_____

_____

_____

FOR SPIRITUAL BLESSINGS:

_____

_____

_____

FOR TEMPORAL BLESSINGS:

_____

_____

_____

Day Six: Supplication

Now with your heart prepared before God, let your requests be made known to Him. The Apostle John tells us that if we ask anything according to God's will, He hears us. The following is a prayer that reflects the heart of God for you, as revealed in scripture.

A Prayer for a Pure Heart

Eph. 3:14-20. I bow my knees to the Father of our Lord Jesus Christ (and ask) that He would grant you, according to the riches of His glory, to be strengthened with might through His Spirit in the inner man, that Christ may dwell in your hearts through faith; that you being rooted and grounded in love, may be able to comprehend with all the saints what is the width and length and depth and height and to know the love of Christ which passes knowledge; that you may be filled with all the fullness of God. (KJV)

Lord, I pray that according to the riches of your grace, I may be led by your Spirit so much so that Jesus would be at home in every corner of my heart; that I may know truly that he loves me and that I may experience the extent of that love so that the full measure of your presence would flood my soul.

Record your personal requests along with the date in the space below so you can keep track of God's faithfulness.

_____

_____

_____

_____

_____

_____

_____

_____

_____

_____

_____

_____

_____

_____

_____

"The secret of all failure is our failure in secret prayer."

The Kneeling Christian

Day Seven: Adoration

Ps. 95:1-7. I come to sing for joy to you, O Lord; I shout aloud to the Rock of my salvation. I come before you with thanksgiving and extol you with music and song. For you, O Lord are the great God, the great King above all gods. In your hands are the depths of the earth, and the mountain peaks belong to you. The sea is yours, for you made it, and your hands formed the dry land. I will come and bow down and worship, I will kneel before my LORD and maker; for you are my God and I am a sheep in your pasture, a sheep under your care. * (NIV)

Ps. 96:1-4, 8-9. I sing to you LORD a new song; I sing to you LORD with all the earth. I sing to you LORD and praise your name; I proclaim your salvation day after day. I declare your glory among the nations, your marvelous deeds among all peoples. For great are you LORD and most worthy of praise. I will ascribe to you, O LORD, glory and strength. I will ascribe to you the glory due your name; I bring an offering and come into your courts to worship you in the splendor of your holiness; to tremble before you with all the earth. For you O Lord, are the Most High over all the earth. * (NIV)

If there is a word or phrase in these verses that especially speaks to your heart today, underline or highlight it and spend a few minutes meditating on its truth.

*Changed from third person to first person

DAY SEVEN: CONFESSION

Confession of your sin is necessary to remove anything that would hinder your prayers to God. Begin with a call for God's help.

Out of the depths I cry to you, O LORD; O Lord, hear my voice. Let your ears be attentive to my cry for mercy. Search me, O God, and know my heart; test me and know my anxious thoughts. See if there is any offensive way in me, and lead me in the way everlasting. (NIV) Ps. 130:1-2; 139:23-24

Identifying and acknowledging your sin before God can be difficult and painful. However, that is the only path to ultimate victory. Below is a list of sins recorded in the Bible. (These are defined for you in detail on page 94). Ask God to show you which ones you struggle with and confess them to Him.

Father, I confess my sins of:

Anger	Malice	Bitterness
Greed	Covetousness	Envy
Gossip	Lying	Stealing
Murder	Fornication	Adultery
Pride	Worldliness	Boasting
Drunkenness	Gluttony	Drug Abuse
Pornography	Lust	Idolatry
Unnatural affection	Evil Thoughts	Impatience
Foul Language	Laziness	Worry
Little Faith	Sorcery	Selfishness
Contentiousness	Unforgiving	Ingratitude
Critical Spirit	Abuse	Hypocrisy
Defrauding Your Spouse		

Use the space provided below to make notes and chart your progress.

Personal Notes and Progress

_____

_____

_____

_____

_____

_____

_____

_____

There is complete forgiveness in Christ and a cleansing of all unrighteousness. Let's repeat a prayer from scripture in response to God's grace.

Ps. 145:8, 9, 18, 21 The LORD is gracious and compassionate, slow to anger and rich in love. The LORD is good to all; he has compassion on all he has made. The LORD is near to all who call on him, to all who call on him in truth. My mouth will speak in praise of the LORD. Let every creature praise his holy name for ever and ever. (NIV)

Father, I thank you for your forgiveness in Christ and, by your Spirit, I pray you will give me a hatred for my sins and the power to repent of them.

DAY SEVEN: THANKSGIVING

G od loves a thankful heart and there is so much to thank him for.

For freedom from the Law: Father, thank you that the Gospel of Grace has delivered me from the condemnation the law demands of those who break it; that in Christ, who kept the whole law, the righteousness of the law is fulfilled in me as I walk in the Spirit

For Identification with Christ: Father, thank you that my salvation has so joined me to Christ that I am identified with Him in every way; His righteousness, His sonship, His inheritance, His eternal life and the object of the Father's love.

For the trials of life: Father, thank you for the trials of life because I know they strengthen my faith as I learn to trust patiently in you. Thank you for your promise to pray for me amidst the storm so my faith will not fail but will be found unto praise, honor and glory at the appearing of Jesus Christ.

For Direct Access: Father, thank you that through Christ I can come freely into your presence with boldness and complete confidence. Even as a child bursts into its parent's room, may I not hesitate to enter your throne room without fear or inhibition.

For Adoption: Father, thank you for adopting me into your family, giving me the full rights of a child of God and guaranteeing me an inheritance in heaven that is incorruptible, undefiled and does not fade away.

God's will is that His children give thanks in everything. 1Thess. 5:18 states that in the midst of any given situation, we are to find reason to be grateful. In other words, Count your blessings...name them one by one:

FOR WHO GOD IS:

_____

_____

_____

FOR WHAT GOD HAS DONE:

_____

_____

_____

FOR SPIRITUAL BLESSINGS:

_____

_____

_____

FOR TEMPORAL BLESSINGS:

_____

_____

_____

Day Seven: Supplication

Now with your heart prepared before God, let your requests be made known to Him. The Apostle John tells us that if we ask anything according to God's will, He hears us. The following is a prayer that reflects the heart of God for you, as revealed in scripture.

A Prayer for Deeper Faith

Habakkuk 3:17-19. Though the fig tree does not bud and there are no grapes on the vines, though the olive crop fails and the fields produce no food, though there are no sheep in the pen and no cattle in the stalls, yet I will rejoice in the LORD, I will be joyful in God my Savior. The Sovereign LORD is my strength; he makes my feet like the feet of a deer, he enables me to go on the heights. (KJV)

Lord, we live in a cursed world that lies in the lap of the evil one; where sin and wickedness dominate and pain and hardship invade our lives. During these times, I pray that you would increase my faith to trust you in spite of my circumstances. I pray that I might view the difficulties of life from the eternal perspective; knowing that any present suffering is temporary and is working in me a far more exceeding and greater weight of glory. Help me to find my joy in you; in your wisdom and your goodness and in the comfort of your promise never to leave or forsake me.

Record your personal requests along with the date in the space below so you can keep track of God's faithfulness.

_____

_____

_____

_____

_____

_____

_____

_____

_____

_____

_____

_____

_____

_____

_____

"We must begin to believe that God, in the mystery of prayer, has entrusted us with a force that can move the Heavenly world, and can bring its power down to earth."

Andrew Murray

"Four things let us ever keep in mind: God hears prayer, God heeds prayer, God answers prayer and God delivers by prayer."

E. M. Bounds

DAY EIGHT: ADORATION

Ps. 105:1-5, 7. I will give thanks to you LORD, and call on your name; I will make known among the nations what you have done. I will sing to you and tell of all your wonderful acts. I will glory in your holy name; let the hearts of those who seek you, O LORD rejoice. I will look to you LORD for your strength; I will seek your face always. I will remember the wonders you have done, your miracles, and the judgments you pronounce. You are the LORD my God; your judgments are in all the earth. * (NIV)

Ps.108:1, 3-5. My heart is steadfast, O God; I will sing and make music with all my soul. I will praise you, O LORD, among the nations; I will sing of you among the peoples. For great is your love, higher than the heavens; your faithfulness reaches to the skies. Be exalted, O God, above the heavens, and let your glory be over all the earth. (NIV)

Ps.111:1-4. Praise the LORD. I will extol you LORD with all my heart in the council of the upright and in the assembly. Great are your works O LORD; they are pondered by all who delight in them. * (NIV)

2Samuel 7:22 How great you are, O Sovereign LORD! There is no one like you, and there is no God but you. Praise and glory and wisdom and thanks and honor and power and strength be to you my God for ever and ever. Amen!" Rev. 7:12 * (NIV)

If there is a word or phrase in these verses that especially speaks to your heart today, underline or highlight it and spend a few minutes meditating on its truth.

*Changed from third person to first person

Day Eight: Confession

Confession of your sin is necessary to remove anything that would hinder your prayers to God. Begin with a call for God's help.

Remember, O LORD, your great mercy and love, for they are from of old. According to your love remember me, for you are good, O LORD. For the sake of your name, O LORD, forgive my iniquity, though it is great. Look upon my affliction and my distress and take away all my sins. (NIV)
Ps. 25:6, 7b, 11, 18

Identifying and acknowledging your sin before God can be difficult and painful. However, that is the only path to ultimate victory. Below is a list of sins recorded in the Bible. (These are defined for you in detail on page 94). Ask God to show you which ones you struggle with and confess them to Him.

Father, I confess my sins of:

Anger	Malice	Bitterness
Greed	Covetousness	Envy
Gossip	Lying	Stealing
Murder	Fornication	Adultery
Pride	Worldliness	Boasting
Drunkenness	Gluttony	Drug Abuse
Pornography	Lust	Idolatry
Unnatural affection	Evil Thoughts	Impatience
Foul Language	Laziness	Worry
Little Faith	Sorcery	Selfishness
Contentiousness	Unforgiving	Ingratitude
Critical Spirit	Abuse	Hypocrisy
Defrauding Your Spouse		

Use the space provided below to make notes and chart your progress.

Personal Notes and Progress

_____

_____

_____

_____

_____

_____

_____

_____

There is complete forgiveness in Christ and a cleansing of all unrighteousness. Let's repeat a prayer from scripture in response to God's grace.

Ps. 19:14; Ps. 25:4-5. May the words of my mouth and the meditation of my heart be pleasing in your sight, O LORD, my Rock and my Redeemer. Show me your ways, O LORD, teach me your paths; guide me in your truth and teach me, for you are God my Savior, and my hope is in you all day long. (NIV)

Father, I thank you for your forgiveness in Christ and, by your Spirit, I pray you will give me a hatred for my sins and the power to repent of them.

Day Eight: Thanksgiving

G od loves a thankful heart and there is so much to thank him for.

For God's promises: Father, thank you for your many promises that are relevant to every possible situation in life and are all yes and amen in Christ; and thank you that each promise is mine to appropriate by faith.

For the Gospel: Father, thank you for the good news, the Gospel of Jesus Christ which is your power for salvation to everyone who believes.

For Angels: Father, thank you for your angels who are ministering spirits sent forth to watch over and protect me against the terror by night or the arrow that flies by day.

For Supernatural Faith: Father, thank you for a faith that sees beyond this life. A faith that enables me to believe in the person and work of Jesus Christ to the degree that it effects my mind, heart and will and ushers me into your kingdom.

For the Scripture: Father, thank you for the Bible, your gift to mankind to impart wisdom and bring guidance and happiness, blessing and prosperity to every soul that studies and obeys its precepts. Thank you that it is also a mirror to my soul that discerns the true thoughts and intent of my heart.

God's will is that His children give thanks in everything. 1Thess. 5:18 states that in the midst of any given situation, we are to find reason to be grateful. In other words, Count your blessings...name them one by one:

FOR WHO GOD IS:

_____

_____

_____

FOR WHAT GOD HAS DONE:

_____

_____

_____

FOR SPIRITUAL BLESSINGS:

_____

_____

_____

FOR TEMPORAL BLESSINGS:

_____

_____

_____

Day Eight: Supplication

Now with your heart prepared before God, let your requests be made known to Him. The Apostle John tells us that if we ask anything according to God's will, He hears us. The following is a prayer that reflects the heart of God for you, as revealed in scripture.

A Prayer of Commitment

John 17:24-26. Father, I desire that they also, whom you have given me, may be with me where I am, to see my glory that you have given me because you loved me before the foundation of the world. "O righteous Father, even though the world does not know you, I know you, and these know that you have sent me. I made known to them your name, and I will continue to make it known, that the love with which you have loved me may be in them, and I in them. (ESV)

Father, I pray that you would open the eyes of my faith to see and appreciate your majesty and your infinite nature which knew me before the creation of the world and then drew me into the grace of salvation. Fill me with the certainty of the glory that awaits me in heaven so I may endure any hardship and any affliction that is a result of my stand for Christ. I pray that I would be sensitive to the intercessory prayers of Jesus on my behalf giving me the opportunity, the desire and the boldness to share your immeasurable love to a lost and dying world.

Record your personal requests along with the date in the space below so you can keep track of God's faithfulness.

_____

_____

_____

_____

_____

_____

_____

_____

_____

_____

_____

_____

_____

_____

_____

_____

"If you are bent on prayer, the devil will not leave you alone. He does not mind our praying about things if we leave it at that. What he minds, and opposes steadily, is the prayer that prays on until it is prayed through, assured of the answer."

Mary Warburton Booth

Day Nine: Adoration

P*s. 111:3-4, 10b. O LORD, glorious and majestic are your deeds, and your righteousness endures forever. You have caused your wonders to be remembered; You, O LORD are gracious and compassionate. To you alone belongs eternal praise. * (NIV)*

*Ps.135:1,3,5,6,7. I will praise your name O LORD; I will praise your name. I will call upon all your servants to give you praise; for you, dear LORD are good. I will sing praise to your name, for that is pleasant. I know that you, O LORD are great, that you are greater than all gods. You do whatever pleases you, in the heavens and on the earth, in the seas and all their depths. You make clouds rise from the ends of the earth; you send lightning with the rain and bring out the wind from your storehouses. I revere your name dear Father and praise your wondrous glory * (NIV)*

Ps. 9:1-2. I will praise you, O LORD, with all my heart; I will tell of all your wonders. I will be glad and rejoice in you; I will sing praise to your name, O Most High. (NIV)

If there is a word or phrase in these verses that especially speaks to your heart today, underline or highlight it and spend a few minutes meditating on its truth.

*Changed from third person to first person

DAY NINE: CONFESSION

Confession of your sin is necessary to remove anything that would hinder your prayers to God. Begin with a call for God's help.

O LORD, do not rebuke me in your anger or discipline me in your wrath. For your arrows have pierced me, and your hand has come down upon me. Because of your wrath there is no health in my body; my bones have no soundness because of my sin. My guilt has overwhelmed me. Ps. 38:1-4a (NIV)

Identifying and acknowledging your sin before God can be difficult and painful. However, that is the only path to ultimate victory. Below is a list of sins recorded in the Bible. (These are defined for you in detail on page 94). Ask God to show you which ones you struggle with and confess them to Him.

Father, I confess my sins of:

Anger	Malice	Bitterness
Greed	Covetousness	Envy
Gossip	Lying	Stealing
Murder	Fornication	Adultery
Pride	Worldliness	Boasting
Drunkenness	Gluttony	Drug Abuse
Pornography	Lust	Idolatry
Unnatural affection	Evil Thoughts	Impatience
Foul Language	Laziness	Worry
Little Faith	Sorcery	Selfishness
Contentiousness	Unforgiving	Ingratitude
Critical Spirit	Abuse	Hypocrisy
Defrauding Your Spouse		

Use the space provided below to make notes and chart your progress.

Personal Notes and Progress

_____

_____

_____

_____

_____

_____

_____

There is complete forgiveness in Christ and a cleansing of all unrighteousness. Let's repeat a prayer from scripture in response to God's grace.

Ps. 32:1, 2, 5. Blessed is he whose transgressions are forgiven, whose sins are covered. Blessed is the man whose sin the LORD does not count against him and in whose spirit is no deceit. Then I acknowledged my sin to you and did not cover up my iniquity. I said, "I will confess my transgressions to the LORD "—and you forgave the guilt of my sin. (NIV)

Father, I thank you for your forgiveness in Christ and, by your Spirit, I pray you will give me a hatred for my sins and the power to repent of them.

Day Nine: Thanksgiving

God loves a thankful heart and there is so much to thank him for.

For Life: Father, thank you for the profound gift of life. For every breath, for every step, for every smile, for every touch; for every day that I wake and realize that you love me and brought salvation to my soul.

For Hope: Father, thank you for the hope that you have placed in my heart for those things yet unseen; things like the redemption of my body, the second coming of Jesus Christ and the glory that awaits me in the new heavens and the new earth.

For Heaven: Father, thank you for heaven, my eternal home. Thank you that Jesus is even now preparing a place for me in a city that has streets of gold and gates of pearl, a river of life with trees whose leaves are for the healing of the nations and where the Glory of God is her light and there are no more tears and no more sorrow.

For the Armor of God: Father, thank you for the full armor of God that protects my mind and heart against the attacks of the evil one and gives me the only effective weapon to defend against any potential stronghold in my life.

For God's omniscience: Father, what a blessing to know that you know all things. You know every word that I speak and every thought that I think. You know my heart which is turned toward you and desires to please and obey you even when I fail and fall into temptation.

God's will is that His children give thanks in everything. 1Thess. 5:18 states that in the midst of any given situation, we are to find reason to be grateful. In other words, Count your blessings...name them one by one:

FOR WHO GOD IS:

_____

_____

_____

FOR WHAT GOD HAS DONE:

_____

_____

_____

FOR SPIRITUAL BLESSINGS:

_____

_____

_____

FOR TEMPORAL BLESSINGS:

_____

_____

_____

DAY NINE: SUPPLICATION

Now with your heart prepared before God, let your requests be made known to Him. The Apostle John tells us that if we ask anything according to God's will, He hears us. The following is a prayer that reflects the heart of God for you, as revealed in scripture.

A Prayer for Discerning Love

Phil. 1:9-11. And this I pray, that your love may abound still more and more in knowledge and all discernment, that you may approve the things that are excellent, that you may be sincere and without offense till the day of Christ, being filled with the fruits of righteousness which are by Jesus Christ, to the glory and praise of God. (KJV)

Lord, I pray that I would learn to love with a Godly love. I pray that I would grow in knowledge and discernment to recognize the highest and the best. I pray that I might live my life blameless and without offense serving you by the power of Jesus Christ to the glory of your name.

Record your personal requests along with the date in the space below so you can keep track of God's faithfulness.

_____

_____

_____

_____

_____

_____

_____

_____

_____

_____

_____

_____

_____

_____

_____

_____

"Each time, before you intercede, be quiet first, and worship God in His glory. Think of what He can do, and how He delights to hear the prayers of His redeemed people. Think of your place and privilege in Christ, and expect great things!"

Andrew Murray

Day Ten: Adoration

P*s. 145:3-7. You are great dear LORD and most worthy of praise; your greatness no one can fathom.* One generation will commend your works to another; they will tell of your mighty acts. They will speak of the glorious splendor of your majesty, and I will meditate on your wonderful works. They will tell of the power of your awesome works, and I will proclaim your great deeds. They will celebrate your abundant goodness and joyfully sing of your righteousness. (NIV)*

Ps. 145:8-13. You dear LORD are gracious and compassionate; slow to anger and rich in love. You are good to all; you have compassion on all you have made. All you have made will praise you, O LORD; your saints will extol you. They will tell of the glory of your kingdom and speak of your might, so that all men may know of your mighty acts and the glorious splendor of your kingdom. Your kingdom is an everlasting kingdom, and your dominion endures through all generations. You, Father are faithful to all your promises and loving toward all you have made. Let every creature praise your holy name for ever and ever. * (NIV)

If there is a word or phrase in these verses that especially speaks to your heart today, underline or highlight it and spend a few minutes meditating on its truth.

*Changed from third person to first person

Day Ten: Confession

Confession of your sin is necessary to remove anything that would hinder your prayers to God. Begin with a call for God's help.

I wait for you, O LORD; you will answer, O Lord my God. I confess my iniquity; I am troubled by my sin. O LORD, do not forsake me; be not far from me, O my God. Come quickly to help me, O Lord my Savior. Ps. 38:15, 18, 21-22 (NIV)

Identifying and acknowledging your sin before God can be difficult and painful. However, that is the only path to ultimate victory. Below is a list of sins recorded in the Bible. (These are defined for you in detail on page 94). Ask God to show you which ones you struggle with and confess them to Him.

Father, I confess my sins of:

Anger	Malice	Bitterness
Greed	Covetousness	Envy
Gossip	Lying	Stealing
Murder	Fornication	Adultery
Pride	Worldliness	Boasting
Drunkenness	Gluttony	Drug Abuse
Pornography	Lust	Idolatry
Unnatural affection	Evil Thoughts	Impatience
Foul Language	Laziness	Worry
Little Faith	Sorcery	Selfishness
Contentiousness	Unforgiving	Ingratitude
Critical Spirit	Abuse	Hypocrisy
Defrauding Your Spouse		

Use the space provided below to make notes and chart your progress.

Personal Notes and Progress

_____

_____

_____

_____

_____

_____

_____

There is complete forgiveness in Christ and a cleansing of all unrighteousness. Let's repeat a prayer from scripture in response to God's grace.

Ps. 51:10, 12, 17. Create in me a pure heart, O God, and renew a steadfast spirit within me. Restore to me the joy of your salvation and grant me a willing spirit, to sustain me. The sacrifices of God are a broken spirit; a broken and contrite heart, O God, you will not despise. (NIV)

Father, I thank you for your forgiveness in Christ and, by your Spirit, I pray you will give me a hatred for my sins and the power to repent of them.

Day Ten: Thanksgiving

God loves a thankful heart and there is so much to thank him for.

For my Suffering: Father, I hate suffering but help me to view it with eternity in mind so that I may be thankful in the midst of my affliction knowing that it is working for me a greater weight of glory.

For an eternal Inheritance: Father, thank you for an eternal inheritance that is too wonderful for my senses to comprehend, reserved for me in heaven, rich with your Glory and abundant beyond imagination.

For God's keeping power: Father, thank you that you chose me and called me and adopted me into your family and that now no power in the universe can take me from the security of your love.

For Fellowship with the Saints: Father, thank you for the fellowship of all my brothers and sisters who are in Christ; bound together by one spirit in one body by a common faith that unites us in a common hope which is the foundation of our ministry to one another.

For truth: Father, thank you for your truth that is perfect, without error and is a lamp to my feet and light to my path in the midst of a dark world filled with duplicity and deceit.

God's will is that His children give thanks in everything. 1Thess. 5:18 states that in the midst of any given situation, we are to find reason to be grateful. In other words, Count your blessings...name them one by one:

FOR WHO GOD IS:

_____

_____

_____

FOR WHAT GOD HAS DONE:

_____

_____

_____

FOR SPIRITUAL BLESSINGS:

_____

_____

_____

FOR TEMPORAL BLESSINGS:

_____

_____

_____

DAY TEN: SUPPLICATION

Now with your heart prepared before God, let your requests be made known to Him. The Apostle John tells us that if we ask anything according to God's will, He hears us. The following is a prayer that reflects the heart of God for you, as revealed in scripture.

A Prayer for Christ-likeness

Psalm 25:1-7. To you, O LORD, I lift up my soul; in you I trust, O my God. Do not let me be put to shame, nor let my enemies triumph over me. No one whose hope is in you will ever be put to shame, but they will be put to shame who are treacherous without excuse. Show me your ways O LORD, teach me your paths, guide me in your truth and teach me, for you are God my Savior, and my hope is in you all day long. Remember, O LORD, your great mercy and love; for they are from of old. Remember not the sins of my youth and my rebellious ways; according to your love remember me, for you are good, O LORD. (NIV)

Lord, I pray that each day I would grow more sensitive to the leading of the Holy Spirit as He guides me to the center of your will. I pray that you might give me a holy hatred for the sins in my life that still appeal to me and seek to draw me into their control. Help me to experience the freedom I have in Christ through the victory He secured at the cross and let me rejoice in my God who loves and forgives me while changing me from one level of glory to the next.

Record your personal requests along with the date in the space below so you can keep track of God's faithfulness.

_____

_____

_____

_____

_____

_____

_____

_____

_____

_____

_____

_____

_____

_____

"If the Christian does not allow prayer to drive sin out of his life, sin will drive prayer out of his life. Like light and darkness, the two cannot dwell together."

M.E. Andross

"Prayer will make a man cease from sin, or sin will entice a man to cease from prayer."

John Bunyon

Sins Defined

Anger: Have you lost your temper with anyone or do you have a spirit of indignation or resentment in your heart?

Malice: Do you harbor ill will toward anyone or anything? Do you wish harm or pain to come to another person?

Bitterness: Do you have a sprit of contempt or animosity toward anyone or anything?

Greed: Do you have a selfish or excessive desire for something beyond your need?

Covetousness: Are you jealous of anyone for what they have and wished that you had it?

Envy: Do you have a strong desire to possess what someone else has and are willing to take it away from them?

Gossip: Do you talk about anyone behind their back especially concerning personal issues? Do you spread rumors or listen to those that do?

Lying: Have you neglected to tell the truth or withheld fact to mislead or deceive?

Stealing: Have you taken anything that did not belong to you or kept anything that belonged to someone else?

Murder: Have you had any desire in your heart or have you wished for someone's death?

Fornication: Have you been involved in any sexual activity with another person outside the boundaries of marriage?

Adultery: Have you been intimate with another married person other that your spouse or have you entertained the idea of such a relationship in your heart? Have you looked upon someone other than your spouse with longing or desire?

Pride: Do you struggle with submitting to God or to others? Do you have a sense of self-sufficiency and/or are you egotistical?

Worldliness: Do you have an inordinate desire for the things that this world has to offer? Are you consumed in your thinking as to how you might acquire them?

Boasting: Do you brag, glory or exalt yourself or someone you know so as to lift yourself or them above another?

Drunkenness: Do you consume alcohol to the point of becoming light headed or intoxicated?

Gluttony: Do you overindulge or binge when you eat? Are your thoughts constantly on the next meal that you are going to have?

Drug Abuse: Do you take illegal drugs or abuse prescription drugs?

Pornography: Have you exposed yourself to explicit sexual images of any sort for the intent of being stimulated?

Lust: Do you harbor an intense desire for something or someone that is not within the guidelines set by God?

Unnatural affections: Are you involved with or do you have a desire or fantasize about having an intimate relationship with a member of the same sex?

Foul Language: Do you curse or use the Lord's name in vain? Do you listen to or share inappropriate conversations with others?

Idolatry: Is there anything or anyone at all that you hold in higher esteem than God?

Evil thoughts: Do you entertain any thoughts that are displeasing to God and pleasing to the Devil?

Impatience: Do you become agitated or upset when things don't go according to your time table? Are you visibly irritated and annoyed when there is a delay?

Laziness: Do you have an unhealthy desire for ease and inactivity? Is it difficult to motivate you to complete a task in an expedient and timely fashion?

Worry: Are you anxious about the future or about things that you have no control over? Do you fret about your circumstance to a point of mental distress?

Little Faith: Do you struggle with believing in who God is, what he has done and what his promises are? Do you have difficulty in trusting him in all the circumstances of your life? Do you doubt Him when there is affliction or suffering?

Sorcery: Are you involved in witchcraft, fortune telling, séances, divination or horoscopes? Do you seek power or assistance in any way from evil sources?

Selfishness: Are you concerned excessively or exclusively with yourself: seeking or concentrating on your own advantage, pleasure, or well-being without regard for others?

Defrauding your spouse: Are you withholding emotional, physical or sexual intimacy from your spouse without mutual consent?

Unforgiving: Are you holding a grudge toward someone who has wronged you and are unwilling to let go of your anger or contempt?

Contentiousness: Do you strive with others, bickering and arguing about details, viewpoints or perspective without grace or understanding?

Ingratitude: Do you lack a thankful heart? Do you feel that you deserve more than what you have or that what you have is not sufficient?

Critical spirit: Are you prone to find fault in people and/or circumstances and do you complain about these perceived faults?

Abuse: Do you mistreat anyone physically, emotionally or verbally with a condescending or hurtful intent?

Hypocrisy: Is your Christian walk and Christian attitude consistent with your faith in Jesus Christ? Do you give the appearance of righteousness while within your heart you delight in wickedness?

Where Do I Go From Here?

You may finish working through this book but you will never come to "The End". Instead it is just "The Beginning". The beginning of a life that is walking in harmony with God, experiencing an intimacy that few Christians experience, and living a life of confidence, inner joy and unwavering hope. These are just a few of the benefits of a consistent lifestyle of proper Biblical Prayer.

It is not the intent of this book to make you dependent upon it so that your prayer life consists of simply reading through the daily prayers. It is meant to be a training tool teaching you the proper pattern of prayer so your prayers are honoring to God and effective in accomplishing His will. This will be evident when prayer becomes a reflex and reading scripture becomes a catalyst to even more prayer.

The next several pages are filled with scriptures related to specific topics. Hopefully they will help you to present your requests using the promises of God that encompass any need you may have.

If there is any one truth that I hope you learn from this book, it is this: No matter how long you are a believer, you will never achieve "success" in your walk with Jesus Christ without the daily exercise of Bible reading and prayer. This is the foundation of *The Faith* and the only means of growing in grace and knowledge. Learn this truth and embrace it wholeheartedly and there are no limits to how God can use you and bless you.

TOPICS FOR PRAYER

The most effective prayers are ones in response to God's word. Here are some topics for prayer that may apply to you. Read the scripture and then pray them back to God. *(All verses quoted from the NIV)*

Children: Sons are a heritage from the Lord, children a reward from him. Ps. 127:3 Train a child in the way he should go, and when he is old, he will not turn from it. Prov. 22:6. Parents do not exasperate your children; instead, bring them up in the training and instruction of the Lord. Eph. 6:4.

Fear: For God did not give us a spirit of fear, but a spirit of power, of love and of self-discipline. 2Timothy 1:7. Be strong and courageous. Do not be afraid or terrified because of them, for the LORD your God goes with you; he will never leave you nor forsake you. Deut.31:6

Comfort: Praise be to the God and Father of our Lord Jesus Christ, the Father of compassion and the God of all comfort, who comforts us in all our troubles, so that we can comfort those in any trouble with the comfort we ourselves received from God. 2Cor. 1:3-4.

Contentment: I have learned to be content whatever the circumstances. I know what it is to be in need, and I know what it is to have plenty. I have learned the secret of being content in any and every situation, whether well fed or hungry, whether living in plenty or in want. I can do everything through him who gives me strength. Phil. 4:11-12. Keep your lives free from the love of money and be content with what you have, because God has said, "Never will I leave you; never will I forsake you." So we say with confidence, "The Lord is my helper; I will not be afraid." Heb.13:5-6

Daily walk: Blessed is the man who does not walk in the counsel of the wicked or stand in the way of sinners or sit in the seat of mockers. But his delight is in the law of the LORD, and on his law he meditates day and night. Ps.1:1-2. Do not let this Book of the Law depart from your mouth; meditate on it day and night, so that you may be careful to do everything written in it. Then you will be prosperous and successful. Joshua 1:8

Decisions: Therefore, I urge you, brothers, in view of God's mercy, to offer your bodies as living sacrifices, holy and pleasing to God—this is your spiritual act of worship. Do not conform any longer to the pattern of this world, but be transformed by the renewing of your mind. Then you will be able to test and approve what God's will is—his good, pleasing and perfect will. Romans 12:1-2

Deliverance: But thanks be to God that, though you used to be a slave to sin, you wholeheartedly obeyed the form of teaching to which you were entrusted. You have been made free from sin and have become slaves to righteousness. Now that you have been set free from sin and have become slaves to God, the benefit you reap leads to holiness, and the result is eternal life. Romans 6:17, 18, 22

Discernment: I will ask the Father, and he will give you another Counselor to be with you forever—the Spirit of truth. And when he, the Spirit of truth, comes, he will guide you into all truth. Jn.14:16; 16:13. But you have an anointing from the Holy One, and all of you know the truth. The anointing you received from him remains in you, and you do not need anyone to teach you. But as his anointing teaches you about all things and as that anointing is real, not counterfeit—just as it has taught you, remain in him. 1Jn. 2:20.27

Finances: Do not worry, saying, 'What shall we eat?' or 'What shall we drink?' or 'What shall we wear?' For the pagans run after all these things, and your heavenly Father knows that you need them. But seek first his kingdom and his righteousness, and all these things will be given to you as well. Therefore do not worry about tomorrow, for tomorrow will worry about itself. Each day has enough trouble of its own. Mat. 6:31-36. And my God will meet all your needs according to his glorious riches in Christ Jesus. Phil. 4:19

Giving: Whoever sows sparingly will also reap sparingly, and whoever sows generously will also reap generously. Each man should give what he has decided in his heart to give, not reluctantly or under compulsion, for God loves a cheerful giver. 2Cor. 9:6-7.

Growth: ..being confident of this, that he who began a good work in you will carry it on to completion until the day of Christ Jesus. Phil. 1:6. for it is God works in you to will and act according to his good purpose. Phil. 2:13.

Guidance: Whether you turn to the right or to the left, your ears will hear a voice behind you, saying, "This is the way; walk in it." Isa. 30:21

Healing: Is any one of you sick? He should call the elders of the church to pray over him and anoint him with oil in the name of the Lord. And the prayer offered in faith will make the sick person well; the Lord will raise him up. If he has sinned, he will be forgiven. Therefore confess your sins to each other and pray for each other so that you may be healed. The prayer of a righteous man is powerful and effective. Ja.5:14-16.

Holiness: Therefore, prepare your minds for action; be self-controlled; set your hope fully on the grace to be given you when Jesus Christ is revealed. As obedient children, do not conform to the evil desires you had when you lived in ignorance. But just as he who called you is holy, so be holy in all you do; for it is written: "Be holy, because I am holy." 1Peter 1:13-16.

Hope: May the God of hope fill you with all joy and peace as you trust in him, so that you may overflow with hope by the power of the Holy Spirit. Romans 15:13. We wait in hope for the LORD; he is our help and our shield. In him our hearts rejoice, for we trust in his holy name. May your unfailing love rest upon us, O LORD, even as we put our hope in you. Ps. 33:20-22

Joy: I have set the LORD always before me; Therefore my heart is glad, and my whole being rejoices; You make known to me the path of life; in your presence there is fullness of joy; at your right hand are pleasures forevermore. Ps. 16:11.

Marriage: Each man should have his own wife, and each woman her own husband. The husband should fulfill his marital duty to his wife, and likewise the wife to her husband. The wife's body does not belong to her alone but also to her husband. In the same way, the husband's body does not belong to him alone but also to his wife. Do not deprive each other except by mutual consent and for a time, so that you may devote yourselves to prayer. Then come together again so that Satan will not tempt you because of your lack of self-control. 1Cor.7:2-5

Singleness: It is good for a man not to marry. But each man has his own gift from God; one has this gift, another has that. An unmarried man is concerned about the Lord's affairs—how he can please the Lord. An unmarried woman or virgin is concerned about the Lord's affairs: Her aim is to be devoted to the Lord in both body and spirit. 1Cor.7:32

Patience: Be patient, then, brothers, until the Lord's coming. See how the farmer waits for the land to yield its valuable crop and how patient he is for the autumn and spring rains. You too, be patient and stand firm, because the Lord's coming is near. James 5:7-8. There is a time for everything, and a season for every activity under heaven: Ecc.3:1.

Perseverance: Therefore, my dear brothers, stand firm. Let nothing move you. Always give yourselves fully to the work of the Lord, because you know that your labor in the Lord is not in vain. 1Cor.15:58. Consider it pure joy, my brothers, whenever you face trials of many kinds, because you know that the testing of your faith develops perseverance. Perseverance must finish its work so that you may be mature and complete, not lacking anything. Blessed is the man who perseveres under trial, because when he has stood the test, he will receive the crown of life that God has promised to those who love him. James 1:2-4,12.

Security: For I know whom I have believed, and am convinced that he is able to guard that which I have entrusted unto him against that day. (2Tim. 1:12) Now unto him who is able to keep you from falling and to present you before his glorious presence without fault and with great joy; to the only God our Savior be glory, majesty, power and authority, through Jesus Christ our Lord, before all ages, now and forevermore! Amen. (Jude24-25)

Thoughts: The weapons we fight with are not the weapons of the world. On the contrary, they have divine power to demolish strongholds. We demolish arguments and every pretension that sets itself up against the knowledge of God, and we take captive every though to make it obedient to Christ. 2Cor. 10:4-5.

Temptation: So, if you think you are standing firm, be careful that you don't fall! No temptation has seized you except what is common to man. And God is faithful; he will not let you be tempted beyond what you can bear. But when you are tempted, he will also provide a way out so that you can stand up under it. 1Cor. 10:12-13.

O LORD, I call to you; come quickly to me. Hear my voice when I call to you. Set a guard over my mouth, O LORD; keep watch over the door of my lips. Let not my heart be drawn to what is evil, to take part in wicked deeds with men who are evildoers; let me not eat of their delicacies. Keep me from the snares they have laid for me, from the traps set by evildoers. Let the wicked fall into their own nets, while I pass by in safety. Ps.141:1-4,9-10.

Speech: Do not let any unwholesome talk come out of your mouths, but only what is helpful for building others up according to their needs, that it may benefit those that listen. Eph. 4:29. Speak to one another with psalms, hymns and spiritual songs. Sing and make music in your heart to the Lord, always giving thanks to God the Father for everything, in the name of our Lord Jesus Christ. Eph. 5:19-20

Suffering and affliction: Now if we are children, then we are heirs—heirs of God and co-heirs with Christ, if indeed we share in his sufferings in order that we may also share in his glory. For I consider that our present sufferings are not worth comparing with the glory that will be revealed in us. Romans 8:16-17.

For our light and momentary troubles are achieving for us an eternal glory that far outweighs them all. So we fix our eyes not on what is seen, but on what is unseen, since what is seen is temporary, but what is unseen is eternal. 2Cor. 4:17-18

Verses on Adoration

Psalm.9:1-2
1 Chronicles 29:11
Psalm.18:1-3A, 30.
2Samuel 7:22
Nehemiah 9:6
Psalm.29:1-2
Psalm.36:5-7
Psalm.57:7-11
Psalm.62:1, 6-8
Psalm.63:1-5, 7-8
Psalm.73:25-26
Psalm.84:1, 2, 4, 10-12
Revelation.7:12
Psalm.18:31-32
Psalm.24:1-2
Psalm.28:6-7
Psalm.34:1-3
Psalm.66:1-4
Psalm.71:1, 15-16, 19, 23-24
Psalm.73:25-26
Psalm.89: 1, 2, 5-8, 11-15
Psalm.92:1-5, 8
Psalm.95:1-7
Psalm.96:1-4, 8-9
Psalm.105:1-5, 7
Psalm.108:1, 3-5
Psalm.111:1-4
Psalm.135:1, 3,5,6,7
Psalm.145:1-13
Psalm.147:1, 3, 4, 7-12
Psalm.148:1-6, 13
1Chronicles.16:8-14, 23-34

Verses on Confession

Psalm.139:23-24
Psalm.51:1-4, 9
Psalm.30: 1,2,4,11,12
Psalm.51:10
Psalm.19:14
Psalm.25:4-5
Psalm.86:11-16
Psalm.25:6, 7b, 11,18A
Psalm.38:1-4a
Psalm.32:1, 2, 5
Psalm.38:15, 18, 21-22
Psalm.51:12, 17
Psalm.79:9
Psalm.54:1-2
Psalm.103:8, 10-13
Psalm.130:3-7
Psalm.30:5, 11, 12
Psalm.130:1-2
Psalm.139:23-24
Psalm.145:1, 9, 18, 21
Psalm.103:8, 10-13

VERSES ON THANKSGIVING

Ephesians.2:8-9
2Corinthians. 9:8
Deuteronomy.7:9
Lamentations.3:22-23
Ephesians.2:4-5
Romans.8:38-39
Philippians.4:19
Isaiah.65:24
Philippians.1:6; 2:12
Ephesians.3:20
1Corinthians. 2:12-13
2Timothy. 1:12
Jude 24-25
Colossians.1:16-17
John 14:16&26
Ephesians.1:13-14
Psalm 19:1
Psalm 33:6&9
Jeremiah.32:17
Psalm 19:7-11

VERSES ON SUPPLICATION

Ephesians.1:17-19
Ephesians.3:14-20
Philippians.1:9-11
Colossians.1:9-11
Hebrews.13:20-21
Psalm.4:1
Psalm.5:1-2, 3b
Psalm.17:1, 3b, 6
Psalm.86:3-5
Psalm.86:6, 7, 10
Psalm.54:1-2
Psalm.143:1, 7a, 8